Baby Talk

🔂 Dominie Press, Inc.

A sheep's baby is a lamb.
It goes baa, baa, baa.

A goat's baby is a kid.
It goes maa, maa, maa.

A dog's baby is a puppy.
It goes wuff, wuff, wuff.

A cat's baby is a kitten.
It goes meow, meow, meow.

A hen's baby is a chick.
It goes cheep, cheep, cheep.

A duck's baby is a duckling.
It goes quack, quack, quack.

When I was a baby,
I went goo, goo, goo!